Solar System

DATE DUE	

PHOTO CREDITS: Cover: PhotoDisc. 1, 3, 4, 5, 6, 8, 10, 11: National Aeronautics and Space Administration (NASA); 12: PhotoDisc; 14: NASA; 15: Dembinsky Photo Associates/Richard Hamilton Smith; 16: PhotoDisc; 17, 18: NASA; 19, 20: PhotoDisc; 21, 22, 23, 24, 25, 26, 27, 28, 30: NASA; 31: PhotoDisc; 32, 33: NASA; 35: Photodisc; 36, 37, 38, 39, 40, 41, 42: NASA; 43: Photodisc; 44, 45: NASA.

The images on the cover and title page are composite images, made up from more than one photograph. They have been artificially colored.

Library of Congress Cataloging-in-Publication Data available.

ISBN 0-439-38247-5

Book design by Kay Petronio

15 14   07

Printed in the U.S.A.   23

First trade printing, October 2002

We are grateful to Francie Alexander, reading specialist, and
to Adele M. Brodkin, Ph.D., developmental psychologist, for their
contributions to the development of this series.

Our thanks also to our science consultant Ralph Winrich
of NASA's Glenn Research Center.

We live on a spinning, revolving **planet**
called Earth. Earth belongs to a very
large family of nine planets and more
than ninety **moons**. At the center
of this family is the Sun. The entire
family is known as the **solar system**.

Cooler areas on the surface of the Sun appear as dark spots.

At night, we see thousands of **stars**. During the day, we see only one, the Sun. The Sun is a star. The Sun looks much larger and brighter than the night stars because it is millions of times closer to us than the stars we see at night.

THE SUN

The Sun is the center of the solar system. It is very big. If it were hollow, you could fit more than one million Earths inside of the Sun.

Explosions of gas flare up from the Sun's surface.

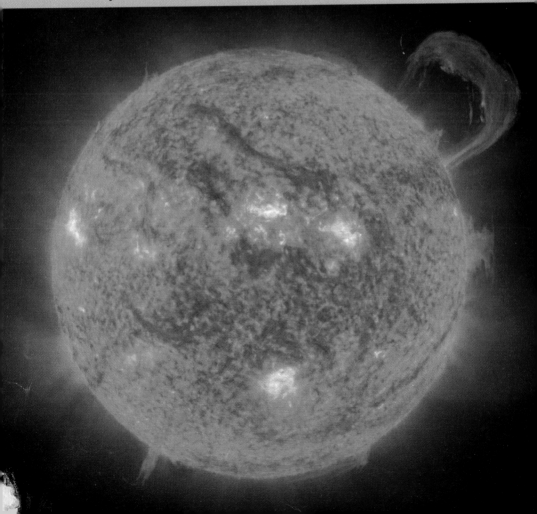

SUN	
Size Across	864,970 miles (1,392,000 kilometers)
Rotation (one complete spin)	24 to 34 days (The Sun's middle spins faster than its north and south poles)
Composition	Hydrogen, Helium
Temperature	Surface: 6,400° F (3,571° C) Center: 15,000,000° F (8,333,316° C)

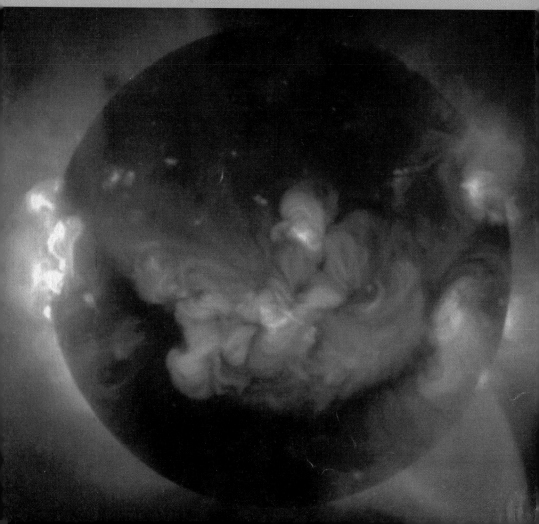

The Sun has **gravity**. Gravity is a force that attracts all objects to one another. The Sun's gravity pulls on the planets and moons. Gravity makes the planets and moons travel around the Sun. They follow paths called **orbits**. The Sun's gravity keeps the solar system together.

The Sun is very hot. It is made of gas. Deep inside, hydrogen gas is squeezed and heated to 15,000,000°F (8,333,316°C). It is turned into helium gas. When this happens, energy is released. It flows out from the Sun as light and heat. This is what we see and feel.

An X-ray view of the Sun's surface

MERCURY

Mercury is one of the smallest
planets. It is closest to the Sun. This
makes Mercury very hot. The side of
Mercury facing the Sun gets twice as
hot as a kitchen oven—800°F (427°C).
The dark side is three times colder
than Antarctica in winter—minus
297°F (minus 183°C).

Mercury is a rocky planet. It doesn't have air. The air around a planet is also called an **atmosphere** (**at**-muhss-fihr). Mercury doesn't have water, either.

Mercury's surface looks like the surface of Earth's moon. There are thousands of bowl-shaped holes called craters. These craters were made when space rocks smashed into Mercury.

MERCURY	
Size Across	3,031 miles (4,880 kilometers)
Distance from the Sun	35,340,000 miles (56,872,662 kilometers)
Orbit Length (once around the Sun)	87.66 days
Rotation	58.66 days
Number of Moons	None
Number of Rings	None

VENUS

The second planet from the Sun
is Venus. It is nearly as large as Earth.
Venus is always covered with white
clouds. The air around Venus is
poisonous. The clouds are made of
tiny drops of acid. The Sun's heat
passes through the clouds and
is trapped at the surface.

*Maat Mons, a volcano on Venus, in an image created
from data collected by the Magellan spacecraft*

Size Across	7,520 miles (12,102 kilometers)
Distance from the Sun	67,239,000 miles (108,207,000 kilometers)
Orbit Length (once around the Sun)	226.4 days
Rotation	243 days
Number of Moons	None
Number of Rings	None

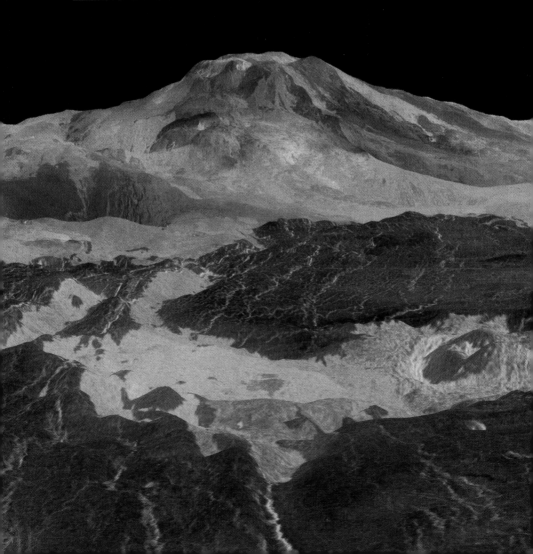

Trapped heat makes Venus the hottest planet. Metals like lead and zinc would melt on its surface.

Venus is made of rock that comes from volcanoes (vol-**kay**-nohz). The surface is covered with lava.

How do we know about Venus when we can't see its surface? **Astronomers** (uh-**stron**-uh-merz) are scientists who study objects in space. They use spacecraft to study Venus. A spacecraft is a machine that rockets to other planets. The *Magellan* spacecraft traveled to Venus. It sent radio waves through the clouds. Astronomers studied how the waves bounced back. This told them what the surface of Venus was like.

A view of Venus provided by Magellan. *The black spaces are gaps in the data.*

EARTH

We live on the third planet from the Sun. Our home is mostly covered with water. The land is made of rock and soil. It has mountains, valleys, and broad plains. Some of the land is always covered with ice.

Nearly everywhere you look are living things. Earth is home to millions of plants and animals. They live on the land, in the oceans, and in the air.

EARTH

Size Across	7,926 miles (12,756 kilometers)
Distance from the Sun	93,000,000 miles (149,000,000 kilometers)
Orbit Length (once around the Sun)	1 year
Rotation	24 hours
Number of Moons	1
Number of Rings	None

A volcanic eruption photographed by astronauts aboard a space shuttle

Lots of air surrounds Earth. Winds blow white clouds across the surface. The clouds are made of water drops. Eventually, the drops fall as rain or snow. Water runs across the land and wears it away. Volcanoes spew out lava to make new land. Earth is constantly changing.

EARTH'S MOON

One moon travels around Earth. It is called the Moon. The Moon is made of gray and black rock from volcanoes. Sunlight bouncing off the Moon makes its surface look white. The Moon's surface is pitted with millions of craters. The crater Copernicus is 58 miles (93 kilometers) wide.

Astronauts orbiting the Moon took this photograph of Earth.

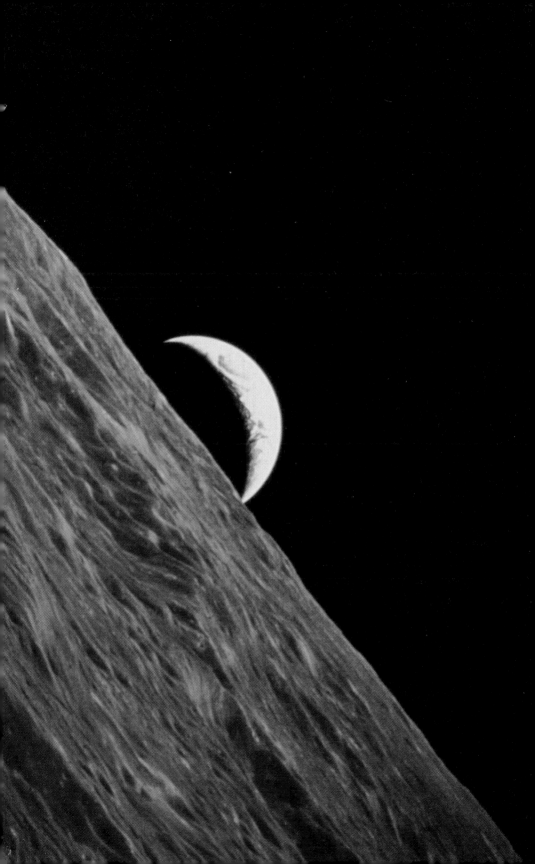

In 1969, the first humans set foot on the Moon. They were called astronauts. They wore space suits containing air because the Moon has no atmosphere. Astronauts brought back moon rocks. Astronomers studied the rocks to learn how the Moon was formed.

Astronaut Buzz Aldrin on the surface of the Moon

In 1971, astronaut James Irwin worked on the Lunar Roving Vehicle.

Astronomers think the Moon was created billions of years ago during a collision. An object the size of the planet Mars collided with Earth. Earth was smaller then. Most of the object joined with Earth to make it bigger, but a chunk flew off. This became the Moon. It has orbited, or circled, Earth ever since.

MARS

Mars, the fourth planet from the Sun, is reddish. Its surface is covered with rusty-colored rock and dust.

Mars has a giant canyon that makes Earth's Grand Canyon look tiny by comparison. The canyon on Mars is longer than the distance across the United States.

An image of Mars taken by a space telescope

MARS	
Size Across	4,220 miles (6,794 kilometers)
Distance from the Sun	141,732,000 miles (228,089,300 kilometers)
Orbit Length (once around the Sun)	1.88 years
Rotation	24.62 hours
Number of Moons	Two
Number of Rings	None

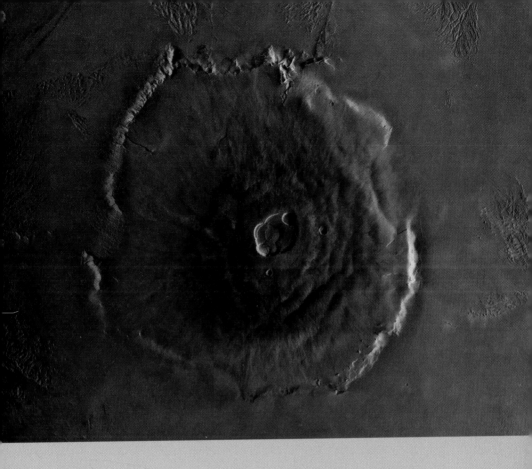

Mars also has very large volcanoes. The volcano Olympus Mons is three times higher than Mt. Everest on Earth. Mars has a thin atmosphere surrounding it, but there is not enough air for humans to breathe. If you went there, you would have to wear a space suit to live.

This image shows a vehicle called a rover, which will be sent to explore Mars in the future.

One of Jupiter's moons passes across its surface.

JUPITER

Jupiter, the fifth planet from the Sun, is the first of four giant planets. It is made of gas and is eleven times wider than Earth. Large clouds travel around Jupiter.

The clouds are mostly orange and white. Winds blow the orange clouds in one direction and the white clouds in another. This makes Jupiter look like it has stripes!

Jupiter has a huge storm that swirls like clouds in a hurricane (**hur**-uh-kane) on Earth. The storm is twice the size of Earth.

Great Red Spot

Callisto

Ganymede

JUPITER

Size Across	88,849 miles (142,984 kilometers)
Distance from the Sun	483,879,000 miles (778,706,470 kilometers)
Orbit Length (once around the Sun)	11.86 years
Rotation	9.92 hours
Number of Moons	28 (possibly more)
Number of Rings	3

Astronomers have given the storm on Jupiter a name—the Great Red Spot.

Jupiter also has many moons orbiting it. Two of these moons, Ganymede and Callisto, are larger than the planet Mercury. Another moon has erupting volcanoes on its surface. Two other moons are ice-covered, with oceans of water beneath.

This image combines several photographs to show Jupiter and four of its moons.

SATURN

Saturn, also a giant gas planet, is the sixth planet from the Sun. It has thousands of narrow rings circling it. The rings are made of rock, ice, and dust. They can be seen with telescopes from Earth. The other giant planets have rings, too, but they are much smaller and harder to see.

Saturn's clouds are the color of butterscotch.

Saturn's rings are made up of thousands of narrow rings. The colors in this photograph were changed by a computer to make the rings easier to see.

SATURN

Size Across	74,900 miles (120,536 kilometers)
Distance from the Sun	888,615,000 miles (1,430,048,100 kilometers)
Orbit Length (once around the Sun)	29.46 years
Rotation	10.66 hours
Number of Moons	30 (possibly more)
Number of Rings	Thousands

An artist's image of Saturn and some of its moons

More than 30 moons orbit Saturn. Astronomers keep discovering more. One moon, Titan, is very large. It is a few hundred miles (kilometers) wider than Mercury. Titan has a strong gravity that holds an atmosphere of gas. Smaller moons do not have enough gravity to hold atmospheres. The gas surrounding them escapes into space.

URANUS

The third giant planet is Uranus. It is the seventh planet out from the Sun. Uranus is four times larger than Earth. Chemicals in the air make the planet look green.

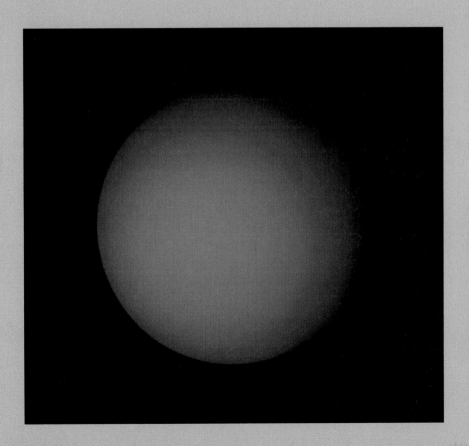

URANUS

Size Across	31,022 miles (49,946 kilometers)
Distance from the Sun	1,787,274,000 miles (2,876,260,000 kilometers)
Orbit Length (once around the sun)	84.01 years
Rotation	17.24 hours
Number of Moons	21 (possibly more)
Number of Rings	11

Uranus is a sideways planet. It spins like all planets but it is tilted on its side. For half its orbit, Uranus's north pole points toward the Sun. For the other half, the south pole points toward the Sun.

Miranda, one of the moons of Uranus

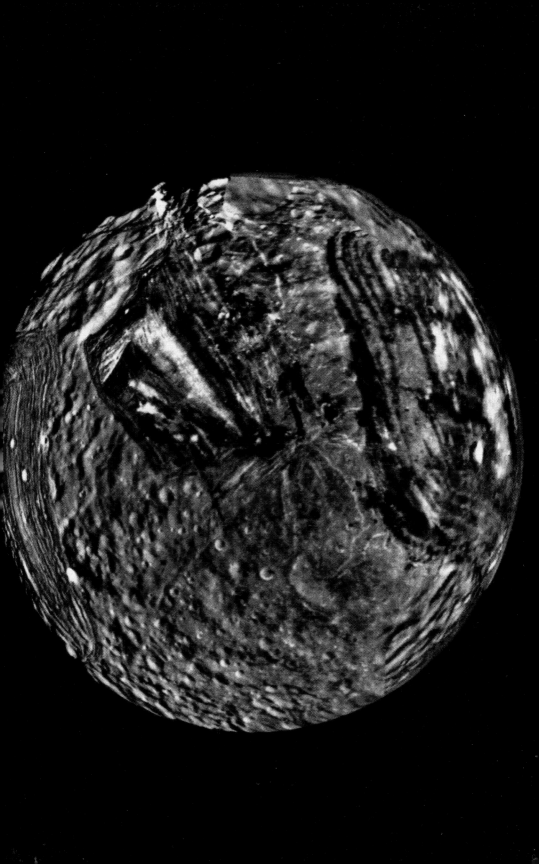

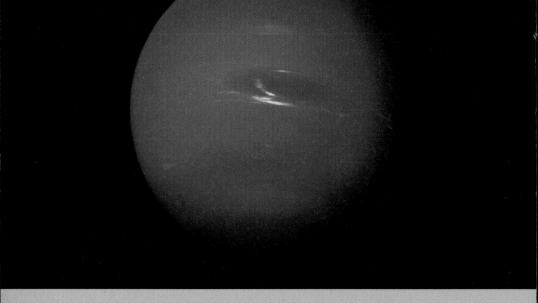

NEPTUNE

Neptune is the last of the giant planets and the eighth planet from the Sun. Blue in color, it is about as large as Uranus. Neptune has storms like Jupiter's, but they are smaller. Occasionally, high white clouds appear in Neptune's air. Winds blow them around the planet at speeds of over 1,200 miles per hour (1,931 kilometers per hour).

The Great Dark Spot is a storm on Neptune.

NEPTUNE	
Size Across	30,236 miles (48,680 kilometers)
Distance from the Sun	2,800,044,000 miles (4,506,110,800 kilometers)
Orbit Length (once around the Sun)	164.8 years
Rotation	16.11 hours
Number of Moons	8 (possibly more)
Number of Rings	6

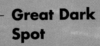

———————— **Great Dark Spot**

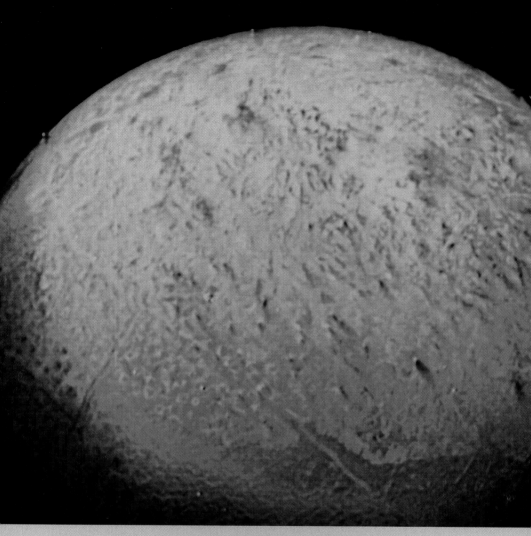

The surface of Triton looks like the outside of a cantaloupe melon.

Neptune has several moons. The biggest is Triton. Astronomers have noticed that Triton is getting closer to Neptune. Millions of years from now, Triton could smash into Neptune.

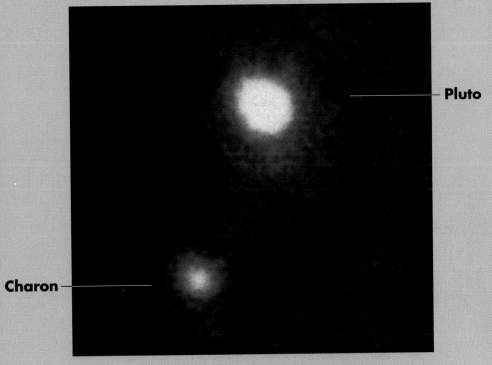

Pluto and its moon, in a photo taken
by a space telescope

PLUTO

The smallest planet is also the last planet in the solar system. Pluto is made of rock and ice. It has just one moon, named Charon. The moon is half as large as Pluto.

Astronomers don't know much about Pluto because it is so far away. It would take a small spacecraft at least 15 years to travel to Pluto. Pluto looks like a dark, fuzzy dot even in the biggest telescopes. Sunlight on Pluto is 1,500 times dimmer than on Earth.

This drawing shows how a spacecraft used to travel to Pluto might look.

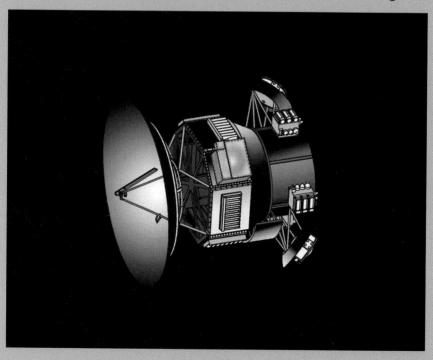

PLUTO

Size Across	1,416 miles (2,280 kilometers)
Distance from the Sun	3,667,827,000 miles (5,902,633,900 kilometers)
Orbit Length (once around the Sun)	247.7 years
Rotation	153.3 hours
Number of Moons	1
Number of Rings	None

Some astronomers think that Pluto is not a planet. They think it is really just a large space rock called an **asteroid**. Other astronomers disagree. Asteroids are shaped like giant potatoes. Pluto is a round object like the other planets.

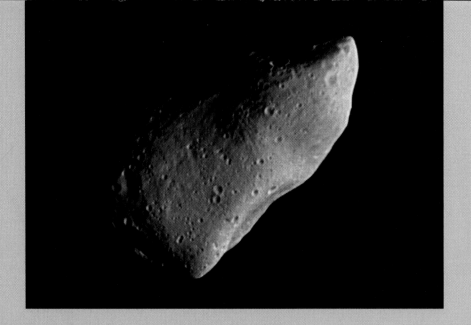

ASTEROIDS AND COMETS

There is still more to our solar system.
Thousands of asteroids orbit the
Sun. Some of these space rocks are
hundreds of miles (kilometers) across.
Others are the size of houses. Many
asteroids orbit the Sun between Mars
and Jupiter.

Far beyond Pluto are billions of large
balls of ice called **comets**. Comets are
usually a few miles (kilometers) wide.
They orbit the Sun very slowly.

Sometimes, a comet will be bumped by another object in space, and the comet will fall toward the Sun. The Sun's heat starts melting the ice. A long white tail of gas streaks out for millions of miles (kilometers). We can see the tail from Earth.

The comet Kohoutek

EXPLORING SPACE

Astronomers study the solar system for many reasons. They use tools like telescopes to look at the planets. They send spacecraft out to visit them. One reason they do this is to find out where the solar system came from. Astronomers think the Sun's family started out as a great cloud of gas and dust in space. Gravity caused the cloud to fall into itself. Most of the cloud became the Sun. Smaller clumps became the planets, moons, and comets.

Another reason to study the solar system is to find out if we are alone. Is there life on another planet? None has been discovered yet. Someday, astronauts will travel out to the planets. Mars will be the first. Building special cities on Mars will make it possible for people to live there. Then there *will* be life on other planets. It will be *us*!

An artist's idea of what an early base on Mars might look like

Glossary

asteroid—a large piece of space rock

astronomers—scientists who study
   objects in outer space

atmosphere—the mixture of gases
   that surrounds a planet

comets—large ice balls that form long
   tails when they near the Sun

gravity—the force that attracts all
   objects to one another

moons—balls of rock or ice that orbit
   planets

orbits—the paths planets travel
   around the Sun

planet—a large ball of rock or gas
   that orbits the Sun

solar system—the family of the Sun,
   planets, asteroids, and comets

stars—huge balls of very hot gas

Index

A Note to Parents

Learning to read is such an exciting time in a child's life. You may delight in sharing your favorite fairy tales and picture books with your child.

But don't forget the importance of introducing your child to the world of nonfiction. The ability to read and comprehend factual material will be essential to your child in school and throughout life. The Scholastic Science Readers™ series was created especially with beginning readers in mind. These books, with their clear texts and beautiful photographs, will help you to share the wonders of science with *your* new reader.

Suggested Activity

Want to find out more about our solar system? A great place to check is the Internet site StarChild. StarChild is brought to you by the National Aeronautics and Space Administration (NASA). It is packed with useful information about and pictures of the Sun, planets, moons, stars, and more. You can also find interesting activities to try, and learn about being an astronaut and how space suits work. StarChild has links to other useful astronomy Internet sites. You can find StarChild at the following address:

http://starchild.gsfc.nasa.gov/docs/StarChild/StarChild.html